The secret of the white buffalo

An Oglala Legend

C.J. Taylor

Tundra Books

1993

May the four directions of the universe live in peace and mutual respect.

Special thanks to Skawennā: Ti Sky

Also by C.J.Taylor:

How Two-Feather was saved from loneliness
The Ghost and Lone Warrior
Little Water and the gift of the animals
How we saw the world: Nine Native stories of beginnings

The winter had been cold and long. The people grew restless waiting for spring. Arguments broke out over who should do the work of the village. Children paid no attention to their parents. Parents lost patience with their children. The elders tried to keep peace but were not listened to.

The elders hoped that the coming of spring would make everyone feel better and stop the arguments. When the buffalo returned, everyone would be busy, cutting and drying meat, stretching, scraping and tanning hides. And there would be feasting and dancing and goodwill.

The weather grew warmer. But the buffalo did not return. Where were they? Scouts must be sent out to look for them.

The two best scouts in the village were Black Knife and Blue Cloud. Both were young and strong and knew the plains and the distant hills. Otherwise, they were very different. Black Knife was selfish and bad-tempered, always complaining, showing off and fighting if he did not get his way. Blue Cloud was kind and good-natured, always ready to help.

The two scouts walked for days but saw no sign of the buffalo herds. "We're wasting our time," Black Knife said. "Let's go back."

Blue Cloud objected. "Our people are depending on us. We must keep searching." As he spoke, he saw footprints on the soft ground, leading toward the hills. "Perhaps someone is lost and needs help," he said.

"We've no time to help someone stupid enough to get lost," Black Knife complained. "Let's go back."

But Blue Cloud walked on, following the footprints, and Black Knife had no choice but to come grumbling after him. If he left Blue Cloud and went back to the village alone, he would never be chosen to scout again.

Suddenly both young men stopped, as they saw someone coming down from the hills. It was a woman. Her long black hair floated around her. Her dress was made of the finest white buckskin and on it were beads of many colors. She was the most beautiful woman either of them had ever seen.

"I want her," Black Knife announced. "I'm going to take her back with me."

"But she may not want to go with you," Blue Cloud protested. "We must respect her."

"Respect!" Black Knife sneered. "She is only a woman. If she doesn't want to come with me, I'll drag her."

"Don't say such a thing," Blue Cloud warned. "She might hear you."

Blue Cloud stared in awe at her beauty. She was like someone from another world. When he found his voice, he said: "Are you lost? Can we help you?"

But the woman ignored him and spoke to Black Knife. "I know what you are thinking," she said. "You want to force me to go with you. I dare you to come and try."

Black Knife lunged toward her. Blue Cloud tried to stop him, but he was too late.

Just as Black Knife was about to touch the woman, a cloud descended.

When the cloud lifted, Black Knife had disappeared. Only his bow and quiver of arrows remained on the ground.

Blue Cloud realized that this was a sacred woman with great powers and he was frightened. Would she make him vanish like Black Knife?

But when the woman spoke to Blue Cloud, her voice was gentle and he lost his fear.

"You are a good man, Blue Cloud. I have a message for you to deliver to your village. Tell your people what you have seen here. Tell them the fighting and the arguing must stop. They must prove they can work together. They must build a great tipi in the center of the village. When it is finished, I will come."

Blue Cloud hurried back to the village and told the elders what had happened. The elders called the people together.

The chief spoke: "You have not listened to us when we tried to make peace among you. Black Knife did not listen and he is gone. If we do not listen, we too may perish. Are you ready to listen now?"

Slowly, one by one, each member of the tribe answered: "Yes."

A change came over the village. Everyone brought something to the tas

Even the children helped. A beautiful tipi of white hide rose before them.

At last the tipi was finished. They had all worked together
without fighting. They gathered to look at what
they had achieved. The chief sat at the entrance to the tipi,
the other elders inside, to wait for the arrival
of the sacred woman.

She walked into the village, singing. A hush fell over
the people. Blue Cloud, watching her, thought she looked
even more beautiful than before. Her hair, lifted
by the wind, floated behind her.

In her arms, she carried a bundle covered with the same white
buckskin as her dress.

The woman entered the tipi. "I am White Buffalo Woman. I have come to bring you a gift."

She knelt in the center of the tipi. Sunlight streamed upon her through the smokehole. The elders sat in a circle around her. At the entrance the people gathered to watch.

The woman placed the bundle in front of her and slowly opened it to reveal a pipe with a buffalo carved on one side. Attached to the stem were twelve eagle feathers tied with sweet grass, and four ribbons: black, white, red and yellow.

The sacred woman of the white buffalo held up the pipe.

"You have shown yourselves to be worthy. Therefore I bring you this pipe." She held it out to the chief and explained:

"The buffalo stands for the earth, our mother who gives us food. The eagle feathers stand for the sky and the twelve moons. The sky is our father who watches over us.

"The ribbons represent the four corners of the world. When you smoke this pipe, you must offer it to each in respect to the earth. The black is for the West whose thunder sends us rain to make the seeds grow. The white is for the North that sends cooling winds. The red ribbon is for the East, the home of the first light. It brings wisdom. The yellow is for the South that gives us summer sun to make the grass grow tall in the fields.

"You have shown yourselves worthy of it by working together in harmony. Use it with peace in your hearts and it will make you prosperous."

White Buffalo Woman handed the pipe to the chief to pass around among the elders. Then she rose and walked out of the tipi. The people separated to let her pass. They watched as she moved through the village and into the fields. Suddenly she began to run, and as she ran, she was transformed into a magnificent white buffalo.

Then, just as miraculously, a herd of buffalo appeared, grazing in the fields beyond the village.

The people treasured the
pipe. Whenever they were
tempted to quarrel among
themselves, they remembered
that only through peace could
they solve problems and
prosper.

Soon they were offering
the pipe to the peoples of
other villages. They explained
its meaning just as
White Buffalo Woman had
explained it to them:
that it must be used with
understanding of what nature
gives and what people must
do in return. They hoped that
its message would spread
west, north, east and south to
the ends of the earth.

The Oglala Sioux

The peace pipe is one of the best-known symbols of Native American culture. It is not only a promoter of peace, but is also said to bring goodwill and health to those who venerate it. The pipe creates an instant bond between people as a symbol of brotherhood and friendship.

The pipe was known throughout the Native world before 1492 and each tribe had its own origin legend. That the Oglala combined their peace pipe origin legend with a buffalo is no surprise. The buffalo was the basis of the domestic economy of the Plains tribes. Everything from tipis to rattles for babies came from some part of the animal. The buffalo was prominent in their magic, art and religion. Because the annual return of the herds was uncertain, a supernatural aura surrounded it. Rituals were performed, prayers offered, and when a buffalo was killed, its spirit was begged forgiveness.

The Oglala Sioux, or Dakota, are members of the Teton branch of the larger Dakota family (the three groups being the Santee, the Yanktonai and the Teton). The Oglala dominated the Seven Tribal Council Fires, a "family" of tribes of the Teton Dakota branch that recognized their kinship and did not declare war on one another. The Blackfoot and Brulé were other prominent members of the Council.

Their territory extended east to the Missouri River, south to Nebraska, west to the Teton Mountains, and north into Saskatchewan, but the Black Hills, in present day South Dakota, were the spiritual center of all Tetons. They were also the setting for this legend. The Hills were guaranteed by treaty until gold was discovered there in the late 19th century. Today, the Oglala and their Dakota family are spread over an area that includes southern Saskatchewan and Manitoba and most of the states between Minnesota and Wyoming. Their influence can be seen by the number of settlements named after the Sioux.

Sources of information: *Indians of the United States* by Clark Wissler; *The Indian Tribes of North America* by John R. Swanton; *The Canadian Encyclopedia*, Volume I.

The secret of the white buffalo is adapted from stories in *Black Elk Speaks* by John G. Neihardt (Washington Square Press) and *Myths and Legends of the Sioux* by Marie L. McLaughlin (University of Nebraska Press).

© 1993 C.J. Taylor

Published in Canada by Tundra Books, Montreal, Quebec H3Z 2N2
Published in the United States by Tundra Books of Northern New York, Plattsburgh, N.Y. 12901

Library of Congress Catalog Number: 93-60551

Distributed in France by Le Colporteur Diffusion, 63670 La Roche Blanche, in the United Kingdom by Ragged Bears Ltd., Andover, Hampshire SP11 9HX, and in Australia by Stafford Books, St. Leonards 2065 N.S.W.

Also available in a French edition, *Le Secret du bison blanc* ISBN 0-88776-322-7

Canadian Cataloging in Publication Data:

Taylor, C.J., 1952 —
    The Secret of the white buffalo
For children.

ISBN 0-88776-321-9

    I. Title

PS8589.A88173S3 1993   j398.2'089'975
C93-090371-4   PZ7.T39Se 1993

Design by Michael Dias

Transparencies by Michel Filion Photographe

Printed in Hong Kong by South China Printing Co. Ltd.

The publisher has applied funds from its Canada Council block grant for 1993 toward the editing and production of this book.

At the request of C.J. Taylor, a portion of the royalties of this book is being donated to the Leonard Pelletier Defense Committee (Canada).